beyond worthy

Jacqueline Whitney

THOUGHT
CATALOG
Books

THOUGHTCATALOG.COM
NEW YORK · LOS ANGELES

THOUGHT
CATALOG
Books

Published by Thought Catalog Books, an imprint of the digital magazine Thought Catalog, which is owned and operated by The Thought & Expression Company LLC, an independent media organization based in Brooklyn, New York and Los Angeles, California.

This book was produced by Chris Lavergne and Noelle Beams. Art Direction by KJ Parish. Special thanks to Bianca Sparacino for creative editorial direction and Isidoros Karamitopoulos for circulation management.

Visit us on the web at thoughtcatalog.com and shopcatalog.com.

Made in the United States of America.

ISBN 978-1-949759-17-4

I've been tiptoeing around my soul, terrified that everything will break if I make this transparent move of opening up; I have inched forward but haven't taken the full step. This journey of mine has been about learning to walk again; I'm learning to stand strong within my soul, facing past experiences I've felt inadequate to open up about until now. It hurts like hell healing and reliving the moments that led me to believe I wasn't beyond worthy of this life anymore.

I must relive moments I don't want to relive if I am going to find healing. I know the strength to acknowledge pain always existed within me. I know the words to explain my pain and the eternal lessons I've learned are aching to be released. Both the strength and words have been on the surface of my skin, not deep within, impossible to find. "I just need more time," said my inner dialog, or maybe I don't. It was just fear suffocating me with the parts of my past I don't want to see again. I must face them if I want to move on.

I want to move on. I want to know what it's like to walk without feeling heavy. This book is me learning to walk again. Just learning to walk is a *really* big step. Even as I am writing, I can feel myself beginning to place my heels on the ground instead of tiptoeing, and it's more comfortable here. My toes are relaxing, walking around my soul with more ease at the reality of my memories.

I know there is power in saying, *this is my truth* and *this is how I am overcoming*. I know I wasn't placed on this Earth to hold my truth inside. It's just a matter of finding those last few morsels of courage to say to my soul, "These are the reasons I stopped believing I wasn't beyond worthy of this life."

Words will forever be my stronghold, my hope, my survival.

I write to feel, and I feel to understand.

I do not understand my world or the world I exist in without words.

I write to exist free

You deserve to exist free.
You can exist free now.

Lean in closely to the words you are about to read. It is highly possible you will need to see at least one sentence.

Your heart will feel lighter, your lungs will ease, and clarity about what your future holds will come.

Light is coming. You are safe. Love has got you.

You don't need to have all the answers. Follow your heart's instincts and let universal fate do the rest.

It's normal to be scared. Life is scary, but not as scary as it seems.

Vulnerability might be the most gentle, intense strength you can obtain. Don't let it contain you. If speaking your truth feels terrifying, dance through fear. Someone needs to hear what you have to say. You deserve to say what you want to say.

You are good enough for people the way you are. You are imperfectly perfect.

You are loved and worthy of being loved closely.

You don't need a lover to survive. You won't be lonely forever.

Someone out there needs your heart to hold forever. You are good enough to be wanted in every way. You are wanted.

You don't have to have society's "ideal look" or have a certain body to be loved. I am not saying this because I have to. I mean it—you are beautiful. You are beautiful because you have a soul like no other. Your soul has purpose no other has.

Take care of yourself where you are right now.

This season of waiting is just that: a season. May you be patient in *all* things.

When your soul feels heavy and your life feels difficult, know that your soul will feel lighter soon. Beyond this darkness, there will be light.

It's completely okay to not be able to explain what you feel or not know what to do next.

You are not your mistakes. You are the lessons you choose to learn through them. Keyword: choice. It is a choice to look for a lesson within every mistake. There is always one or a ton.

Everything is going to be fine. You will find happiness, comfort, and contentment in your life. I know you're looking, but keep looking.

If they are continuously hurting you, it is time to walk away.

The pain of grief will go away. Your loved one is with you in spirit.

Don't try to heal your bleeding hands before they're ready.

You will know when it's time to begin healing. You will know when you have healed.

I don't think you're numbing or hiding from your past when emotionally you need a break from it. Trust your heart. Trust.

You are not alone. You can do it. You are strong and you are capable. Be brave and be bold. You're going to figure your life out. You don't have to figure your life out now.

Rest up.

You are not broken even when you feel you're breaking. You're coming together into all of whom you've been made to be.

If you're making an excuse for something, recognize it now.

If you're too hard on yourself, be more gentle.

At the end of the day you are a human being, and no human being has it all together.

You really are doing better than you may feel you are.

I don't know you, but I am so proud of you.

Above all, hold hope. Hope is evident everywhere.

You're finding these words when you needed to.

I want the whole of me
to be entirely
loving
I want the whole of me
to see all
as one
I don't want to walk
and leave broken pieces
in my footprints
I want to rest on a sunlit bench
gather myself
then walk again holding as many hands
as the world offers me
I want to pick up everyone's pieces
because I am alive
to be entirely loving
so as long as I am breathing
I will love all as if
all hearts are beating
to the same precise
rhythm as mine
as if
all of the world has the same heart
as if world peace is already a reality
if you find this poem
can you promise me
as long as you are breathing
you will hold the hand
of my heart
and walk this life together?
may we be forever loving

You're unfolding
Deep layers of growth
Flowing upon the surface
Every day a layer of becoming
Coming out from the unknowing
Every day, another day to grow yourself
To become ready for all of it to unfold
You're unfolding into everything meant to be
I don't believe everything happens for a reason
But everything that happens can become a reason for growth
You're not failing because life doesn't make sense

You're not hopeless because what you want hasn't come to be yet

The keyword is "yet," because an authentic desire of hope for oneself will always come to be in some way at some time

All times have some blessing concealed in the layers within

All times flow into growth
Forgive
Unfold
You are deeply growing

Words from Love,

I will always believe in who you are

If you don't believe in who you are

Come to me and I'll remind you of you

Who you are is everything we need

You've always been everything we need

People believe in you because even when you don't believe in yourself, you move. With your entire soul, you move along somehow, always finding your way to where you belong. Even if where you are isn't where you want to be, you find peace there. Even when you look back, you still look forward. When you say goodbye, you're still always there. You don't give up on people even when over and over again people are giving up on you. People believe in you because you take care of others more than you take care of yourself. The world says take care of yourself first, but you don't think that way because that's just who you are. You are a natural-born caretaker and heart-healer. Empathy has been carved into your bones. Pain tried to take you, but you made it escape you. You found compassion in the middle of it because you never want anyone to feel the heartache you have felt. You've been someone's angel all along. Selfless isn't a strong enough noun for you. You make people believe in themselves. Thank you for that. Some may say you're naive because you'd even try to find some good in a criminal, but I'd say that's admirable.

Your heart is wide open, soaring with pure beauty and gentleness that touches the hearts of more souls than you know. It's hard to look away from someone whose light fills a room. You are a light that fills every room. You may not like yourself sometimes, but you're so likable. You may not see your beauty, but others do. Don't change who you are for someone you know isn't meant to be in your life. Don't change who you are to fit into the world. Your mind and your body fit perfectly in the space where you are. You belong in the space you are, always. Stay true to who you are because your world needs you. It has always needed someone exactly like you.

There are people you say are perfect. You want to be like them, you try to be like them, but you will never be like them. It has manifested into an unhealthy journey to an unrealistic expectation of yourself. The comparing begins to paralyze your mind, body, and spirit. Whether subconsciously or consciously, it is draining to try to be someone else.

It's unfortunately natural to hold hands with the thoughts that tear you apart, to create fingers pointing at you in your mind, to believe the absolute worst about yourself. To blame yourself for everything.

"It's your fault. You could've been better. It's you that's not attractive enough. It's you that caused them to walk away. It's you that made them do that horrible thing. It's you that's crazy. It's you, you, you." Those are the types of destructive (or even worse) thoughts that consume you.

Please, you must try to believe this: You are the reason they say everything happens for a reason. There is no such nonsense as an accident when it comes to you. No burden is carried in your being. You believe your name is synonymous with burden. You feel terrible about every second your "issues" took out of others' lives. Listen: Humans need humans, and humans want to help humans through their suffering.

Your being is the energy that separates dark, bold, intimidating clouds in the sky. Your bravery awakens desperate sunlight. You have the heart that reflects a single star in the universe wrapped around darkness. The bones and skin and everything in between that holds you together couldn't be more perfectly placed. You are perfect the precise way you are, even though you've never believed it.

No, you've never been a burden. No, you aren't annoying. No, you aren't any "less than" because of the crap you've been through.

You are going to leave footprints in places no one ever believed you would make it.

You are the image of a tragic story turned breathtakingly beautiful.

because of the pain
her mind has forced her to make love with,
her heart has given birth to
an undeniable
special tenderness
to love people
her love
is
her gift to her world

For the one who doesn't feel loved,

You're loved because you are Love.

Your heart holds endless oceans of Love. Your heart is on the horizon. Look up. Immerse into the softness of yourself. You're loved because you're alive. You're still here because you're undeniably supposed to be.

Creativity is Love. Don't hold your art back. Laughter is Love. Be recklessly silly. Faith is Love. Always hold on.

Can you hold yourself tonight? Not in a physical way, but in a delicate, soulful way—use your thoughts to surround you in Love.

Your lungs are made of Love.

Your rib cage protects your heart,
and your heart protects you.

Your soul breathes Love.

Let a breath of Love out and let Love do the rest.

Your existence is a promise of hope;
please keep existing.

we're all just looking for confirmation
that who we are is right
that who we are is okay
that who we are is meant to be
here's me confirming to you
who you are is more than right
who you are is more than okay
who you are is more than meant to be

This is how I find healing. I fall apart into my words. I sit down with my crying soul and fall apart. I force my shaking hands to type and wipe away my tears. I cannot heal unless I open. I must open my pain into the formation of words. This is the only way I know how to be okay. I fall into myself, I fall into my keyboard, because I know I'll be okay.

You must fall apart to heal your heart.

it feels like a rush
but there is no rush
you are a boat taking sail
with miles of waters to surround you
that water is there to hold you up
it will not let you sink
you are not sinking
you are sailing
it feels like a rush
but there is no rush

We choose Light.

That's what survivors of deep pain do to survive.

We choose Light instead.

This is why we can say we are survivors.

We choose Light even when every step to healing in front
of us looks like it's headed to hell;

we choose light

While I wish you never felt the pain you have, your scars, whether physical or mental, hold a power of helping someone in a capacity others cannot. You can help the ones who understand what it feels like to touch the darkness with bleeding hands. Healing happens more strongly when we can relate to another's soul.

Be open.

Your little, huge heart cannot settle. Pulsing with an effort that weakens your airway. Which way do you turn when no way seems right? Which way do you turn when every way is blurry and you're in a hurry to understand now? But you know it never works that way. You never figure out the confusion right away. It just never happens that way.

Time goes by in a blink of an eye. You've heard the expression before, but it never meant more than it does right now. You think you're in the same place—you think no big changes have been made. But I see you blind yourself to the skyscrapers you've filled into your pain-engraved spaces. You touch the sky in places that the airplane you hear going by cannot reach. You've reached a girl you couldn't be before. You met her right after the places you explored meant nothing anymore. Those places that seemed meant to be, the things that slid beneath you, gone before you knew it, out with the old in with the new, they say. How are you supposed to know what to say when the world took almost everything away? This is what I say to all of this... You haven't lost yourself. Be proud of what you have to say. Now you can say you've fought for yourself in a way no one else could. You've stopped your heart from nearly ripping apart. You've seen the peace that passes all understanding. The fire that life exploded almost burnt down the only home you had left—you. But you stopped it before you burned all the way to the bone. You've been saved by waters that have always wanted to save you. You've been saved. Don't look away now. Go that way. The way your heart is going.

She can't feel anything anymore. Her body is going numb from the mental pain. It's like her thoughts are wrapping their bleeding hands around her throat, making it difficult to breathe. It's like her thoughts are pushing her darker and deeper down. Her lungs are filling with nothingness, and her body is being pushed so deep she can't feel anything anymore. It's like the only way to feel again is to break skin.

A blade will never be able to touch the places of your pain you can't reach—only Love. So cry to the heavens; put the blade down, pick up a pen, and write on your body instead. Write "I love you" or "You are beyond worthy." Keep going, angel.

an eye can only cry so much
but a soul
a soul can pour

so when you struggle every day
with being brave
and your confidence is consumed
by the world you breathe in
and it all just brings you down
bring your imagination out
picture a rope
strong enough to hold
your boat of burdens
fight against the tide
dock your heart close to shore
because the fight is always worth life
your strength is always worth life
you're worth life
you're doing just fine
breathe with the rhythm of the wave
you're breathing
what a sign of precious life

you are going to crash
insanely hard
but
you are going to rise
insanely strong
you
make it seem
easier than it is
to come up for air
when the waters
don't want you there
there as in
here
here to touch the souls
of so many
you're insanely strong
you never stop
even when you want to
you tried to make it all stop
but every time you survive
you are always supposed to survive

The more we try to make sense of the memories or the current moment that doesn't make sense, the more we lose ourselves and our healing. There are some experiences that just aren't ever going to make sense, and maybe they're not meant to.

even through
immeasurable pain
she
does
not
quit
with unending persistence
she has shown herself
her undeniable strength
she has learned
persistence is the strength
of going on
even though
in any instance
something could go wrong
fear does not stop her
she
keeps
going
she finds strength in her heart
it is always there
no matter what she must bear
she
is
strong

Words on grace:

When I think of Grace, I think of delicacy—
a gentle touch to the soul.

That's what your soul needs—
a gentle touch that feels like the warmest comfort.

A delicate touch—nothing intense.
You've had too much intensity in your life.
You need a calm tide.

Not a touch from a human—
a touch from Grace.

Grace feels like saying,
"It's okay" when your head is spinning.

Grace feels like saying, "That's enough" when
something isn't right.

Grace feels like saying, "Thank you" even when
everything doesn't feel steady.

Grace feels like taking your heart to bed, lying alone
with yourself, and just simply being grateful to be alive.

I am healing as I write this
you are healing as you read this

let love out and let Love do the rest
let love out and let Love do the rest
let love out and let Love do the rest
let love out and let Love do the rest
that is all and that is everything

The sun is in your eyes; deep warmth is within your body. The world can be so cold, but you, you are *always* a ray of warmth shining across your earth. One ray at a time—you always shine. Your eyes are the windows to your warmth. Open them to let fresh light in. The future is terrifying, yet somehow your light never dims. In the dark of night you are still a light. Your eyes truly hold rays of sunshine no other being glistens. Even when you close your eyes to shut out darkness within you, you open brighter because you are a fighter. Look up. Feel the sun soak in your skin. You are alive to feel and to experience all of life's winds. You are alive; a precious gift, you are. Your heart is a home so tender. On the days you want to close your curtains and stay in bed, choose warmth. Always choose warmth. You embody an energy so powerful. A fire of compassion burns inside of you.

You are all that is warm.

hold the hand of your healing
with deep compassion
hold your pain
in the Light within you
we cannot heal without honest recognition
of our experiences
this
I know
you know
feel all you need to heal
feel thoughts come
but let go of them
with the acknowledgement
that painful thoughts
are just another thought
no matter the pain
they make you feel
your pain is not your identity
hold the hand of your pain
with deep compassion

you are a resilient being
ready for this healing season
repeat the words, "be gentle"
whenever you begin
to be too hard on yourself
floods of pain may come
but you will not remain
in your pain for too long
do not forget your spirit of strength
and angels are with you always
so hold tight
what feels like the fight of your life will subside
you are learning
eternal lessons
be gentle
be gentle
be gentle

your worth is not a fleeting moment
it is not a feeling
it is not in words or numbers
it is not in human relationships or the lack thereof

it is not in aesthetics or praise or status among society's
standards

your worth is at home in the simplest Truth
the Truth that is Love
the Truth that you are a one-of-a-kind being
sprouted in the heart of Love
where your purpose began and never ended
your worth is in eternity
it is a forever truth
your worth is in your beating heart
your beating heart is your truth
you
are
alive

worth is a mirror of deserve
you deserve to be on this beautiful planet
surrounded by the sun and stars and moons
to infinity
to heaven
heaven is within you
you have worth, you are worth,

never ever allow anyone to make you believe you aren't
worth it all

you are worth it all
and one promise I can keep is
to be here, right now
is always well worth it
to stay here
is always well worth it

she is going places
far beyond where her heart can see
some are known
most are unknown
but she trusts
she trusts to the core of her being
she trusts in the One who guides her
she trusts that she is surrounded
by unfailing Love
adventure doesn't scare her
no
she is brutally bold
in the most admirable way
through wide seas
she is always making it
to be the person
she's been made to be

peace
is you
it is the moment
between breaths
it is in the posture of your spine
the warmth of your body
the energy between your skin
it is in the resilience of broken bones
and the cries that shake an avalanche
in you
self-care
is giving yourself
the permission and compassion
to sit alone
and just feel
the aliveness of your body
peace
holds your heart
it is your protector
peace is always
holding out a hand
for your heart to hold
rest in the truth
that you deserve
peace
you are peace
rest in the truth
that all that
is meant to be
will find you

when you feel insecure
and the world
around you
is telling you
to be this way
not that way
to look this way
not that way
to believe in this
not that
to love him
not her
to spend your time
extra wisely
because the world
is running
on a timer

and we
have to have this done
by that time
to be practically perfect
when perfection
is unattainable
you must know
you were made for way more
than the world
repeat to your heart
you were made
for more
repeat to yourself
you are more
than enough
precisely as you are

I am so incredibly sorry
you have felt the
deepness of pain
that you have
I am so incredibly sorry
you know what it feels like
to hold darkness so closely
your light almost goes out
I am so incredibly sorry
your world
became so dark
not being here
felt like the only
way to be okay
recovery may seem so distant but it is not
you are a force of nature
a miracle
you will stand on your mountain and look up
knowing a piece of heaven
mercy is a must during your time of the climb
here now, forgive
here now, show yourself sympathy
for all the darkness you have touched
you will embrace more light

remember
even at night
there is still light

will you dance upon tables
with me
with no music on
turn up the volume
on our hearts
and on the count of five
scream
we're alive

And even though,
she chose Love.

Our job is not to save someone from their pain, but to just simply love. Love is what saves.

Simply, loving is our purpose.

I love nighttime
because the moon
reminds me
Light can still be found
in darkness
and the dark of night
reminds me
beyond this darkness
there will be light
Light is coming

Everything is falling into pieces and those pieces are fitting into the exact places they need to.

It will all be okay.

to the Love
that's greater than all
thank You
thank You for providing and guiding
thank You for protecting
thank You for embracing me with openness
amen

I won't even begin
to try to understand
what you've been through
the hell your soul has seen
the blood your eyes have bled
touching death
dreading being left to survive
surviving in a reality
you hate to call your own
surviving to barely survive
from a distance
I see in you someone
who holds a piece of heaven
I see in you someone
who naturally gives others the strength to hold on
I see in you someone
with world-changing capability
your story is a story not just anyone could live
your strength is undeniable
your story is a story of redemption
your story is a story of miracles
your story is a story of hope
I know you always have an angel
by your side protecting you
I know you were always meant to survive
I know you are meant to be where you are
I have no doubt you will always be okay
I am grateful you exist

You have been created for nothing mediocre. You are meant to tear down walls with your heart, push through oceans with your voice, and love all souls with all of your soul. You were made to love. You were made to stand out with all your differences. Sometimes you lay them down for no one to see, but you were made to wake up your world with your unique qualities for all to see. You are nothing close to mediocre.

The ocean reminds me I'm alive to feel in unpredictable, never consistent rhythms.

It reminds me that it's okay to be loud and soft within the certain way my soul feels. To have a soul that feels intensely is my soft power. I can be soft; I just need the moon to pull me harder at times.

Depending on if the water washes over the sand I walk on, my feet either stay on the surface or sink. When I'm closer to the ocean, I sink deeper than when I'm walking on the pale sand that reflects the color of my skin.

I exhale my breaths with the crashing of the nearest wave. To remind my soul I am one with the ocean. We can breathe together, move together, touch the shore at the same time—as long as I want to.

The ocean reminds me my heart is a moon, the gravity that pulls my emotions further or closer to my shore, my serenity.

Your purpose is on the surface of your heart speaking ever so quietly, yet ever so boldly.

You are here for a purpose. You are purpose.

sit in the silence
with yourself
hear the sound
of peace
the sound of silence
is peace
you inhale and exhale peace

your breath is
a doorway to peace

To the one who feels all of life deeply...

This part of you is a vessel in your heart and it is not a curse, it is a blessing. People like you keep the world beating. People like you hold all souls and even when you feel you can't hold any more, you do. And that is a part of you no one should view as negative, especially you. You are a rarity the world needs.

This vessel is a pathway to peace in certain souls only you can calm.

Without you, compassion wouldn't walk in the shoes of some souls who desperately need it.

People like you send energy out that calms through oceans, keeping a tsunami of waves from crashing over hearts that can't afford any more damage.

When you begin to feel painfully overwhelmed by any darkness roaming the earth, may you remind yourself that your light always shines upon it. Your light may be the only reason certain feet don't stumble through their darkness.

I am not saying you are alone in your light. There is a Source way more powerful than we will ever know here guiding you, protecting you, choosing you to be the light we need.

May you trust your unique Light.

But also—I don't want you to hold on too tightly to the depths you feel. I don't want you to feel responsible for bringing peace and healing to all corners of your world. I know you don't care as deeply as you do for attention. I know it comes from the most genuine, natural place. Don't question the whys of being the way you are. You were made this way for a purpose.

I don't want you to think others need help, either. Thinking others need help places them in a space of being "lesser than" and not already whole. We are all already whole and healed. Brokenness is an illusion that was placed in the inheritance of humanity from day one. The human brain has always created a separation from Perfection.

Through the Love greater than everything, we are everything. We are healed. We are accepted as-is. We are complete.

All we really need to do is try to believe in our hearts that everyone is whole and all they need from us is our love. Some souls only need our love through thoughts and prayers. Others need us to hold their hand tightly through despair and just be there. Be completely in the moment and you will always know what to say.

Trust your light.

You aren't someone people take lightly. People look at you and see heavenly strength. They see someone who has walked through endless oceans without catching a breath. They see someone who has caught their breath time and time again when they were barely holding onto it. You held onto your breath with all the strength you had left, and people see that. People see that you're trying every single day. It's not about what other people see; it's about what you see, but it is comforting to know you're seen. So I am reminding you—you are seen. You are not someone people take lightly. You are heavenly strength.

I hope you know that you don't have to know right now. You don't have to know where to go or what to do. You don't have to know who to be or who to be with. You don't have to know the right answer, because maybe there isn't one. You don't have to know what they're thinking of you, because what other people think doesn't matter in the end. In the end, the love you give and receive is all that matters, I believe. I also believe you are someone other people need around. I believe you are going to do something in your life that no one has done before. I believe you have the ability to walk your soul through waters you don't believe you can get through right now. I believe you will always come out on the other side stronger than before. No matter what you believe about yourself, I hope you know your truth. I hope you know you haven't messed up too much to be forgiven. You haven't been through too much to overcome more. You aren't too much of anything to be less than perfect just the way you are. You aren't any less lovable than someone who seems to be better. You aren't too far gone to go far in this life. This life is unpredictable, and it's scary, but we are always more prepared than we feel.

You don't have to know what you need, but if you need something, say something. You're not needy. You're human. You're allowed to mess up. But don't hold on to guilt and embarrassment for too long. It'll be okay. You're allowed to feel off and take as many breaks as you need. Your biggest responsibility is taking care of yourself. You're allowed to not have your life figured out. You're allowed to be *behind* because where you are is fine. Where you are is where you need to be right now. Work doesn't define you. Grades don't define you. Medication doesn't define you. Anxiety doesn't define you. The past doesn't define you. The future doesn't define you. Relationships don't define you. Words don't define you. Looks don't define you. How you love defines you.

When you're going to a place other than home and it's making you anxious even if you've been there before, breathe deeply constantly. All will be well. It's uncomfortable putting yourself out there. Your body, mind, and spirit take time to adjust to new surroundings. Whether you're there for less than a day or more than a year, the change is subtly or greatly shocking. Grounding yourself through silence going into it is important. Taking the time to nurture your personal energy is important. You hold a light-filled energy that protects and carries you. Sitting down with yourself, speaking truth and affirmation is important. When you need to step away from the crowd, know that you can step away without being judged. When you need alone time, have your alone time and let go of guilt. You don't ever need to feel guilty for doing what's best for you. You place more judgment on yourself than anyone else does. Go to an empty room and breathe and smile thinking about how far you've come. When your mind, body, or spirit start to tense up, focus your thoughts on the exact moment you're in. Notice the details around you. What can you hear? What do you see? What colors do you like? Where is there beauty? Where is there a miracle? Breathe deeply constantly; all truly will be well.

your anxiety will subside
your fear will clear
you will find a peace of mind

Forgive yourself. Forgive yourself for the moments you feel you messed up. Forgive yourself for feeling you need to be a perfect person. Forgive yourself for having anxiety. You are trying your best. You are. Do what is best for you, even if it means making someone upset. You aren't intentionally doing it. Maybe they can't understand what you're experiencing and maybe you can't put into words what you're experiencing. Anxiety isn't worth something you don't have to do. Slow down. Put the sanity of your soul before anything else. Forgive yourself for disappointing someone. Say you are sorry and take another breath forward. Always take another breath forward. You are not taking breaths backward.

Symptoms of depression can leave for a while and come back. You may not understand why; you were fine and then you weren't. Something small can trigger it; the sound of a sentence or the scent of something specific. You feel feelings you don't want to feel, and you can't put those feelings into words. Fatigue takes over and your entire body feels heavy. Every step feels like you're dragging your feet through solid water. What's real doesn't feel real. What's normal to them isn't your normal, and that's frustrating. Your eyes are glassy; tears feel like they're going to flow but they won't. You want to be alone, but you don't. You want distractions, but you can't focus on anything. You're thinking, but you don't know what you're thinking about. That's confusing. Your hair gets knotty from the lack of energy to brush it. Your room gets messy from the lack of energy to clean it. You're either really hungry or not hungry at all. You question whether or not you remembered to take your meds. You freak out. A part of you feels weird that you're on meds or you don't know if you need them. You feel like nobody understands the depths you feel. It's overwhelming. It's scary. It's real. Your feelings are valid. Your chemical imbalance is not your fault. There is nothing wrong with you. While depression can come back after leaving, it does leave. And every time it leaves, it walks a little farther away from you. And one day you will be free from it. You must address it, and you must not numb yourself to it. You must not believe it is stronger than you, because it is not. You are the image of strength.

I know the unknown can feel like dust is filling your lungs. Like you've been waiting for so long to know the answers, but you still don't. And sometimes it's hard to breathe because of it. I know the unknown can make you feel so alone to the point you have to ask someone if you're "just going crazy." I know what it feels like to start to question life itself—*why is it just not working for you? Is it my fault?* (It is no one's fault.) I know sometimes nothing makes sense and everything feels off and wrong. You are growing into a person made for every season. You are ready for change, and change will come for you. Life is constantly preparing you deeply to be the person you need to be. For some reason, you don't need to understand or know right now. Maybe there isn't a solid reason for any of it. Maybe you're just simply growing through the unknown and that is the reason. It's not simple, no, but growth is really important. You are being prepared for something important.

Release your breath if you're holding it.

I am giving my body grace.

You being alive is someone's reason to keep going.

keep going

You know, you can cry if you need to cry.

You don't have to hold it back. You don't have to numb yourself to the emotions that are building up like skyscrapers that will never touch the sky. Numbing yourself isn't protecting yourself. Protecting yourself is giving your heart permission to break so that your soul can touch heaven. You don't have to know why you need to cry. You don't have to know why your breathing is getting heavy and your body is getting tingly. If you can't cry, you don't need to know why. Just be, sweet one, just be. Squeeze your hands together to comfort yourself a little. Hold your chest for a little to comfort yourself. Your mind is a full moon and your emotions are Hawaiian waves. You are an ocean that feels in shallows and depths, and that is okay. You hold life itself inside of you. You hold the weight of the world not only on your shoulders but within every cell of your body. Let go of the unnecessary responsibility to save yourself or anyone else. It is okay to feel changes the way you do. It is okay to feel loneliness like empty space within space. Cool down the wildfire inside of you with a good cry. Do not worry; the ocean that is within you will hold your tears safe and carry you to your peaceful place. Whether it's a few drops down your face or an entire ocean, you will find peace in the shoreline of your precious beating heart.

Please don't think you are what they did to you. You are not. You aren't less valuable because they left you. There's not something wrong with you because they took advantage of you. You aren't the words they spoke to you. You aren't the words spoken about you. You aren't the bruises on your body or the heart they gave you. You aren't trauma. You aren't bad memories. You aren't sin if that word means something to you. You are forgiven. You aren't "less than" anyone. We are all equal.

I want you to know you don't have to hide your heart from someone or something that could potentially be for you because you've been hurt. Moving on and opening up is scary. I hope you give yourself all the space and gentleness you need. The more you do this, the more you will see what you need come to you. Things don't work out in this life when they aren't aligned with your soul's ideal journey. Every soul is a spirit, and every spirit is moving toward something greater than what's understandable. You don't have to understand why something happened or what you *should* be doing now. All you *need* to do is be wholeheartedly loving and you will see all you need show up for you.

Maybe it was never about them deserving you or you deserving them. Maybe they treated you terribly not because they wanted to. Maybe they have a deep pain causing them to act certain ways. It's not an excuse whatsoever, but *compassion is forgiving and forgiving is healing.*

Maybe they left you because they were never meant to be with you. Maybe you didn't date that one person because you were never meant to.

Maybe you don't know what you're supposed to be doing currently because you're meant to let curiosity lead you to knowing your True Self better. Maybe it's not about knowing what to do and it's about the process of figuring it all out, because in the figuring out you can learn so much about so much.

Maybe your struggles aren't for your people to understand because they haven't struggled the way you have. *Not everything in this life is attached to something you did wrong.* Not everything in this life is attached to something wrong with you. Our minds naturally hold on to negativity more than reality. Everything is what it is. Everything isn't the sum of your overthinking. There's usually always a *maybe* that can expand your perspective and help you see any situation in more light.

I'm sending you a breath of air for the spine that you carry and the wings that keep you steady. I'm sending you, through prayer, a lot of love. I imagine you feel light at times but heavy at others. I imagine you don't know where to begin at times but flow through others. I imagine you don't know how to find the words to express how you feel in good ways and in bad ways. I imagine an area of your soul needs to find nurturing words or people to soak in. I can't imagine what it's like to live in that miraculous body you live in, but I can imagine how it keeps you going. I know your body holds you tight when your world is spinning out of control. I know gravity isn't against you and the world isn't, either. I know your body keeps you warm in a society that can be cold. I know your body doesn't want to hurt you. I know a lot of things are messed up around us, but I know there are miracles like you that exist which make me worry less. I know love is the air we must inhale and exhale. I don't know a lot of things, but I do know some things.

The only words she can find is *I'm okay*, but she truly isn't. Lonely, sad, exhausted, confused. How is she supposed to be okay when one thing after another goes wrong? How is she supposed to be okay when she's mentally and physically drained? On the verge of falling apart while desperately trying to keep herself together. Her world is spinning and her heart won't settle. One precious breath at a time, she's trying to go on. She's hurting, but she's trying. And that's how we know she'll be just fine—she tries. She tries to be okay when it's hard. She tries to hold light when it's dark. She tries to see the good in everything terrible. She tries to keep her heart open when the sky is falling. She tries. She will be fine. *You will be fine.*

please believe
there is still time
for you to be
all that you want
to be
there is time

If you're in the middle of overthinking and your thoughts are exhausting, you think about this—nothing at all needs to be perfect. Your thoughts of the future may be realistic, or more likely they're not. You can't plan what will actually happen, and while that is terrifying—you can find comfort still. Maybe you'll feel uncomfortable and anxious, or maybe you won't. Maybe you'll fail completely, or maybe you won't. Maybe you'll feel beautiful, or maybe you won't. Maybe you'll fall in love, or maybe you won't. Nothing at all needs to be perfect or happen perfectly. You can remind yourself your life is unfolding as it needs to. You can remind yourself of the truths you believe in. You can remind yourself you are breathing in this moment and that's what matters most. Your breath holds you steady and you can focus on it when you feel out of control. You can remind yourself you are whole in every moment. You can remind yourself you are doing your best. You can remind yourself you are always growing and healing. You can remind yourself you haven't taken too many steps back. You can remind yourself time isn't against you. When you are overthinking, you are in control of what you choose to think about.

Breathe through your thoughts. Hold on to your heart.
One breath at a time.
You are finding your way.

keep believing
continue breathing
in love
out love
you are succeeding

For her, hope is there, but only in small breaths. With every inhale she feels she's losing herself more with every exhale. With every effort forward, she's more tired after. The back-and-forth of finding reason and then being confused again is tiring. The back-and-forth of finding strength and then feeling tired again is tiring. Finding her way is tiring. Smiling while trying to be okay is tiring. Life is tiring. But even though most is unknown, she knows hope is always there. And that's what gets her through. She never stops believing that even though her efforts may not be showing results now, someday they will. Even though she experiences moments of deep loneliness, she knows that someday she'll be held. Even though hope comes in small breaths, she knows small hope is big hope.

And that's what life does to you. It throws in an almost unbearable hardship or ten and expects you to be okay right away. (Or maybe that was just me expecting to be okay right away.)

And years go by and you're still not okay. Everything feels abnormal and nothing feels right or meant to be. They say what is meant to be will always be, but when you're in the heat of the hardship that is impossible to believe.

The miracle of the pain happens when you accept your situation for what it is. You cannot expect to accept it right away. You won't. You shouldn't. The pain teaches you what it needs to so you can be who you need to and your moment of *yes this is why* won't come when you expect it to. You may even get to a point where you almost forget it must lead to something of importance, and that's when it does. Something happens out of nowhere and you can literally feel your healing escape you. This unexplainable energy leaves your body, and a lightness overcomes you. Someone looks you in the eye and says *I'm proud of you,* and you cry.

You believe to the depths within you that your pain was leading you to purpose all along. You believe to the depths within that your pain was a gift all along. You believe to the depths within that no one truly got you through except you because you had the will to fight. It was you all along who was created for this pain and this purpose. It was you.

The more you surrender to the journey you are clearly on, the more opportunities will come your way. The more you believe in your capabilities and natural gifts, the more opportunities will come your way. The more you are kind to your mind, the more opportunities will come your way. Opportunity comes when we surrender. Surrender means to cease resistance. You must stop resisting the signs that are clearly leading you one way or another. You must stop resisting your visceral reactions. You must stop listening to the voices of others when you know where the voice within you is undoubtedly guiding you. You may doubt, but doubt doesn't always mean no. You will know when the doubt means no; situations won't flow and fear will be clear. Every single one of us has a purpose. Every single one of us has something inherently special that can be used to give life to others and ourselves. If you don't have people who believe in the decisions you believe with everything in you are the right decisions, don't look down. You have it in you to trust and motivate yourself. When your bones are brittle with doubt, I hope you look up and inhale deeply while saying *you can do all the things you believe in*. When your heart is beating with joy, I hope you allow yourself to fully experience it. When you come to a point where you finally realize why you went through what you did, I hope you cry and hug your heart tightly. You deserve this life— my goodness, you deserve this life. You worked harder than anyone will ever know. You've always been soaring. Honestly, you should clap out loud. Give yourself an awkward round of applause, but embrace it. You deserve this life you're molding yourself into.

If you feel like you're shutting down... Rise. As sunshine is promised every day at dawn, your peace is, too. You are surrounded by perfect, clean air. Breathe it in; life is giving you a reason to rise—you are alive. What feels like the most important task to be done right now is not important at all. Your mind, heart, and spirit are always the most important task to take care of. Rise not because you must be here for others—rise because you must be here for yourself. Stop working to please others. Work to find yourself. Work to love yourself. Let go of tasks if you can't handle them right now. Hold on to your heart when you're shutting down. Hold on to your truth. You are wholly deserving of living a life encompassed by peace, love, and joy. You are wholly deserving of finding clarity amongst chaos. Always start with your breath. Your breath is closest to your heart. Your heart is protected by strong lungs, and this is where your breath begins. You are being protected. The answers to what you need are on the surface—far closer than they seem to a tired mind. They aren't deep in there scheming to hide from you. Answers are here, now. Go to your heart and say, *What do you need, sweetheart?*

You are not lost. You are finding.

This is your heart speaking to your brain:
She is free to be
Whoever she wants to be
Let her be

She went numb. She went numb to protect herself from the hell of her reality. She went numb to ignore the bleeding of her soul. She went numb to defy the lies being tethered to her bones. She went numb to survive.

She's confused. Confused as hell about how the hell she got to that place. What the hell carried her there? Did she carry herself? There's no way. Where the hell was God during it? Where the hell was that love that was supposed to protect her? Where the hell was her mind? How can a soul fall so far that it doesn't function as its own? As if this soul died for an amount of time and was living a life of another. A body living an out-of-body experience so far away from its own that it's possible it never happened. But it did. And that's what keeps the bleeding lingering. That's what keeps the soul from finding healing...it did happen. How the hell did it happen to her out of all the souls it could have happened to?

If you are her, I am sorry. Listen to me, read this, you are not crazy. You are not crazy. There is absolutely nothing wrong with you. Forgive yourself. Forgive yourself. You are going to tell stories of miraculous strength. You are going to save other souls from falling to that place you were in. You are going to come to a place where you accept your reality as much as you can, and you will find complete peace. You don't deserve what happened, no. But you are here right now. The definition of a miracle. You will use your trauma to bring much-needed love into existence. I am proud of you and I believe in you.

You're in control of your soul.

You are the sun
someone needs.
You are a sense of hope
for the heart
who forgot
what the sun feels like.

Lately, more than half of the time, her mind is half-functioning to its fullest degree. Her thoughts mostly consist of *why does my brain feel this way?* Exhaustion feels too common. Fogginess as well. Frustration holds her head in a lock. She's trying—with great effort—to unlock a clear mind. She'll straighten her spine for better circulation to her mind. She'll get up after sitting a while to try and walk it off. This helps, but not enough. Caffeine makes her anxious. Sleep helps, but not enough. Exercise helps, but not enough. Nothing seems or feels enough. The day passes, it's six o'clock, and she didn't finish her day's work. "Where did my day go? What did I even do?" Her days have been a blur and it's uncomfortable. Being in public is uncomfortable. Answering the question, "How are you?" is uncomfortable. Her thoughts are beginning to live within her physical body, and pain is showing up. Tension aches in her back. Headaches follow her to bed. She knows she is not crazy, but it sure feels like it sometimes.

For the one who thought *this is me...*

Visualize your mind as a cloud. You are floating in a bright blue sky surrounded by other clouds. These clouds are other minds feeling the same fogginess you've been experiencing. You are not the only one experiencing an unclear mind.

Visualize your breath as a cloud. As you inhale and exhale, your white beauty expands—separating, allowing Light to break through. Light always breaks through when we give ourselves patient space to open up. You *can* find patience in all moments.

This page is for me to declare in large letters to reflect how loudly my heart is yelling these words to the precious eyes reading this...

thank you for being alive

Now, notice the energy of your breathing. Notice its rhythm and its temperature on an exhale. Inhale deeply. Deep breathing opens pathways in your brain. It helps awaken your consciousness, and connection to your consciousness brings natural energy to your brain. When your mind starts to overthink, go to your breath. When your mind collapses in a negative trap, go to your breath. Go to your breath when tension arises. Your breath is a reliable resource for clarity and energy. It is not the answer, but it is highly beneficial.

Visualize your heart beating in a cloud—being held in the safety of its bright white beauty. No matter how your heart is beating, it is held safe in Light. So when your heart is beating uncomfortably, remind yourself darkness doesn't hold you—Light is holding you, always.

We are so tiny compared to the vast Universe. When your mind feels small, picture yourself standing on a single piece of dirt while the Earth is spinning around you and other planets are spinning around the Earth. Look up at the sky. You are surrounded by an infinite amount of space.

Visualizing helps my mind feel less tense and enclosed. When I open my creative perspective, my heart eases up, my mind quiets down, and I experience an energy release.

Place both hands on your heart. Take a breath.

Through a silent thought say,
"Sweet soul, I am sorry I've been really hard on you."
Reply back, "I forgive you."

You are infinity times enough.
You are infinity times enough.
You are infinity times enough.
You are infinity times enough.
You are infinity times enough.
You are infinity times enough.
You are infinity times enough.
You are infinity times enough.
You are infinity times enough.
You are infinity times enough.

The courage you need,
you already have.

You do not need to heal from it all
all at once.

Those feelings you are feeling—
you are never alone in them.

With all of me, I hope you move forward with hope.

I hope you find hope inside your heart because it is there no matter what you may bear. I hope you pray with passion to the heaven that exists in your entire being when you feel blinded by confusion. I hope you trust in all of your capabilities, because your capabilities are endless. I hope you open your heart wider than golden gates. I hope you surrender. Surrender to the journey your soul is on. Flow with it. You are an open ocean—waving, crashing, rising, giving life to all life around you. Thank you for being you.

Your journey is an open ocean. When you close your eyes and see yourself, I hope you see your horizon. I hope you see the endless, breathless beauty of who you are.

You are making it to the horizon of your ocean. Maybe, actually, you've been walking along your horizon this whole time. Maybe, actually, you're not sinking, you're sailing.

I hope you open your heart to possibility. When you are fearful of your future and doubt your abilities, I hope you hold on. Possibility means something is unknown—but there is chance connected to the outcome. Possibility means there is always hope.

I hope you repeat that you are climbing a mountain that has never been touched, but you are making it to the top. You are making it to the top of your personal mountain, and you can climb. Even when it hurts, you're climbing and that is strength.

Healing takes silence and time. The quieting of my mind, my soul's eyes looking inward at the parts of my past leaving shatters of glass bleeding into my present. The heaviness that has thickened my breathing are these memories entrapping me in depression. Depression, darkness, void, untruthful thoughts, the come-and-go of mental-health stability—I'm tired of it. I'm tired of being okay and then not. I'm tired of hearing a dark silent voice telling me suicide is my destiny. It tells me this cycle that has years in the making will never stop. Heaviness, exhaustion, questioning—is hard. Not knowing what decision I'm supposed to make that feels so big for my next step in life is exhausting and it's all making me feel too tired. Tired of this life battling against the war that is in me. I'm dying to break free from the pain that isn't a part of me. I am so heavy, yet Light reminds me that I am never not full of Lightness. It is my time to heal. It is my time to silence my demons, to give my Light the voice it deserves. My voice has quieted. Society is overwhelming. Life is beautiful and life is too short. We are here to be something for others no one else can be. I say I'm tired of it all, but my soul is not tired. My heart is tired, but my soul is awake shining to overcome it all. So a time of silencing stimulation in society is my strength waking up parts of my soul ready to love me. I'm in it. I'm in the intensity of healing and I'm taking it full force. I am not giving my healing half attention; it's got all of me. I write to release. I share to be a hand holding you in your likemindedness.

With all of me, if you lose hope, I hope you fall to your hands and knees and repeat like a broken-hearted record that this is not the end of your journey.

If you lose hope, I hope you place your hands on your heart and say, *"Thank you for keeping me alive, precious beating heart."*

With all of me, I believe in you. I may be a stranger, but all souls exist from the same Love, and that Love connects us. We are connected. We are in this together. I believe in you. Remind someone that you believe in them if you read this.

I hope you hold your past tightly in your hands, but then through focused thought see yourself releasing it. Release the heartaches, the regrets, the traumas, the memories. They may come up again, but with every release they disintegrate more.

You will come to a moment where you realize your past doesn't hold you anymore. And you will cry. And you will notice a new you. Maybe this moment has already happened and you don't even know it. Healing is never as far as it seems. Maybe it's happening right now. A new you is becoming.

Reflect for a moment.

Refresh.

Now breathe forward holding hope in your hands.

When was the last time you sat down in the discomfort of your silence? When was the last time you fell in love with your spirit? Not the spirit of another, but your own worthy energy. Your heart isn't just a heart. Your heart is the source connecting you to everything here on earth. When you're disconnected from you, you're disconnected from everything. It creates a blockage to energy and energy connects us all to all of life. Energy is God. Energy is Love. When you feel this blockage arise and it's uncomfortable to sit alone, begin with where you are. Release judgment against yourself. *I do not judge you for thinking anything that you think.* Feelings and thoughts are just feelings and thoughts. The more time you sit in the discomfort of silence, the more comfortable silence becomes. Silence is always a reliable comfort. Your heart is always a reliable comfort. Humans are unreliable. Within you is where you should always begin. We must make the effort to sit alone, because alone is where we discover our depths. So when life feels lonely, sit alone. Even if it doesn't feel lonely, sit alone. When sitting alone feels uncomfortable, move if you have to, but then go back. You must learn to rely on what's within. It must be a practice. It's normal to become frustrated. Again, release judgment. You'll begin to find your rhythm, your stillness, your creativity. Your rhythm will come and go. If you feel like inspiration is distant, be patient. Sometimes your brain needs a break. Inspiration will show up when you're ready. Your spirit is always looking out for you, and you are a spirit this world needs to experience. May you find patience through your process. Your process is yours to experience. *Experience it.*

For the one in a depressive episode...

Depression is strong, but not stronger than you. There is nothing wrong with you. You are not lazy or crazy. If you feel a lack of motivation for everything, it will pass. Contrary to popular belief, you don't have to be productive all the time. Most of the time, what our minds tell us is productive is just a standard society creates. Most of the time, we don't create the pressure we put on ourselves; society does. Your soul is separate from the world. *Remember that.* You don't have to be on the go all the time. You don't have to constantly move on human schedules. You don't have to live your life day by day if that feels too overwhelming. I always say, go breath by breath. You might cry but not know why. *Let it pour.* You might not want to get out of bed—please stay if that's what makes you feel most okay. You'll know when you're ready to get up. No one else will, *but you will.* You're not being lazy—you're taking care of your brain. If you can't turn an assignment in, don't turn it in. If you had an intense flu you'd take sick days. Take a sick day if you need one. Your brain is recovering. Don't feel like you need to explain to other people how you're feeling. If you need to talk, talk. Don't let this contain you. You'll feel really fragile, but you're not. Depression is an illness, but you're not dying. This isn't the end of the world. The universe isn't against you, so don't be against yourself. Please, if you feel like you are dying—tell someone. If you feel no hope—tell someone. You are worth whatever help you need, and you are never a burden. Hope is translucent to a heart that has been breathing pain, but hope is with you. It's in front of you and it's not as far as it seems. Breath by breath. That is how you'll get through. *You will get through. You always do.*

You've made it to another day, and maybe this day will be your best yet. Maybe this day will be your hardest yet. Or maybe it will be just another day. Either way, you made it to the gift of today and your tomorrows are all gifts, too.

Remind yourself of how far you've come. Your heart has drowned in oceans and climbed its way out of deep waters bringing you back to life. Your heart hasn't given up on your journey. It has continued beating even when you thought it might stop. It continues to beat even when you're not consciously thinking about it beating. How beautiful is your body—it keeps you going without you having to remind it.

Remind yourself of the growth you've made. The situations you can handle now that you were never able to handle before. The situations that caused your walls to cave in are now pillars of strength for you. The more you've spoken up for yourself, the more you've found healing. The more you've put your heart first, the more you've found freedom. Every single seed that becomes a tree of life must break open to begin growing. You have broken to begin growing and you are blooming. You are giving life to the life around you.

Remind yourself of the person you've become. You are no longer someone who lives for themselves. You are someone who lives to love others. The darkness you have lived is now Light for people who desperately need it. The shadows that have followed you are now in front of you serving as wisdom for people who desperately need it. People desperately need your stories.

Remind yourself that you are good enough the exact way you are. The voices of society and the people around you aren't who you are. The opinions of the world aren't who you are.

Remind yourself that you can let go of the past. You don't have to let go right away and you're not meant to feel free right away.

Remind yourself that with all change, Light shows up. Your future is not only bright, but it is also being guided by Light.

Remind yourself you are capable. People will have much to say about the way you're living or the dreams you're planning. You can't always trust people's advice who haven't lived through anything similar to what you have.

Remind yourself you are not what you once did, you are what you do now.

Remind yourself you are worth everything.

Remind yourself it's okay to not be busy all the time.

Remind yourself to not get caught up in being busy.

Remind yourself to take it one thing at a time.

Remind yourself to take your meds if you need them. You're not weak.

Remind yourself it's worth living.

Remind yourself everything cannot happen all at once.

Remind yourself that you always get through. You are here today.

Remind yourself to be kind, regardless.

Remind yourself you're loved beyond your knowledge.

Remind yourself to put yourself before anything else.

I see you and I want to help you.
Be that person.

Sweet soul, I'm sorry it hurts.

Her soul holds other souls. She's the type that gives everyone and anyone a home in her heart. She cares above and beyond unconditionally. She's been to the deepest depths a soul can go, but because of this her heart holds a piece of heaven. She will hold you so peacefully, you will finally feel okay in so many ways. With her around, your soul will make more sense. You'll know her when you meet her.

She's tired. Tired of the pain coming faster than it leaves. She's tired of not knowing why she is the way she is. Tired of putting on a game face when she's fighting a fight no one can see.

She doesn't believe they will believe her. She's supposed to be the happy one, the motivated one, the one who keeps everyone together. Her anxiety is shaking an earthquake in her soul. Depression is drying the ocean within. She tries to shake the negativity. Sometimes just pushes it away or swallows it whole instead of confronting it and moving onward towards healing. Death flirts with her, but she can't leave the ones who love her behind. She knows this, so why does life have to be so damn hard?

The thing about her, regardless of the wounds that go deeper than skin, is that she keeps going. She is strong-hearted, a brave soul you need around. She is trying to heal but needs something she's unaware of to get there.

Ask her how her heart is; hold her in your hands. Her feelings don't make her a burden; tell her. Tell her she's loved beyond the stars. Tell her she can do it. Tell her the world would shake without her strength holding you together. Remind her it's okay to dry her tears on you and that it's okay to reach out and get a little extra help. Don't just tell her she's safe; make her believe it. Love her like you want to be loved. The sun smiles when she does; her heart thrives in the stars, her presence lights up every room. Be a light for her. She's is going to be okay. She is you.

May you meet your soul where it is.

You are not too much, ever.
You've never been too much of anything.

there
is
absolutely
nothing
wrong
with
you

Progress can be measured in breaths.

You are still breathing; therefore, you are making progress.

I feel in my soul
A shift is in control
This shift, destiny colliding
For us all
Through it all
you and I
are becoming who we need to be
In this world and for this world

For the heart beating an anxious pace...

Inhale a deep breath very slowly through your nose and then let it out with force quickly. Do it again. And then do it one more time. Any thought your brain is consuming and running away with doesn't have to be acknowledged right now. Right now, right when you can feel your heart begins to race, you tell your worries they have no place here. They don't need to take up space in your peace. That space of anxiety or overthinking can be replaced with peace. Visualize breathing in peace.

Breathe in peace
Breathe in peace
Breathe in peace

sometimes
the right words
are no words
just love
only love

Being you
is enough.

You don't have to explain yourself to anyone. You don't
have to defend where you are. You are where you are, and
that is where you need to be right now.

We are always searching, we are always changing, we are always learning, we are always finding our way. You aren't lost when you don't know where life is leading you.

You are always stronger than you feel.
You are always more capable than you feel.
You are always more loved than you feel.
You are always less annoying than you feel.

Healing is slow for a reason.

You don't have to work so hard to earn people's love.
You are loved as you are.

You don't have to feel loved to be loved.
You are always loved.

Love will find you. Love is finding you.

You can be the voice you need to hear.

Write something you need to hear on this page and then say it out loud.

You are going to make it through. You will; remind yourself often. Speak to yourself like you're going to make it out of whatever it is you're crawling through, because you will.

You will be ready for whatever outcome may come.

When you read this text someone saying, "I love you and I appreciate you."

your heart carries grace
so let grace carry you

JACQUELINE WHITNEY started sharing her unfiltered thoughts online in 2015 as a way to cope with her struggles. As a teenager, she loved academics and playing volleyball and felt assured about her prospects for the future. Everything suddenly changed when a genetic condition affected her ability to exercise for more than a few minutes at a time. One surgery after another soon followed, with the last operation resulting in a brain injury. Jacqueline loved reading but could no longer read without needing to sleep for hours afterward. After months of trying to finish high school, she decided to withdraw, then persevered to get her GED. Jacqueline then began her long journey to healing. She turned to writing and started sharing her words on Instagram, where thousands experiencing similar struggles continue to be uplifted by her words each day. Sharing her words has provided Jacqueline a unique path to healing, one she hopes will inspire others on their journey to feeling whole again.

These words are for the one looking for hope; for the one questioning whether they'll ever truly be okay. These words are for us all. Hold this book in your hands and hold onto hope. Trust that you will find peace and freedom from your past and clarity for your future. Stop doubting whether you're worthy of living or if continuing to fight for your life is worth it. Pain comes and goes, but with every second, we grow stronger. You will get through whatever it is you are going through. There is hope. Let these words be your guide.

MORE POETRY FROM
THOUGHT CATALOG BOOKS

Your Heart Is The Sea
—Nikita Gill

The Strength In Our Scars
—Bianca Sparacino

Salt Water
—Brianna Wiest

Evergreen
—Kirsten Robinson

**THOUGHT
CATALOG**
Books

THOUGHTCATALOG.COM
NEW YORK · LOS ANGELES